God Is There

**written and illustrated
by Dan Foote**

Equipping Kids for Life

An Imprint of Cook Communications Ministries
Colorado Springs, CO

Faith Parenting Guide
Ages 4-7
Trust

A Faith Parenting Guide
can be found starting on page 32.

Additional copies of this book are available from your local bookstore.

If you have enjoyed this book, or if it has impacted your life,
we would like to hear from you.

Please contact us at:
Cook Communications Ministries
4050 Lee Vance View
Colorado Springs, CO 80918
www.cookministries.com

Faith Kidz is an imprint of Cook Communications Ministries
Colorado Springs, Colorado 80918
Cook Communications, Paris, Ontario
Kingsway Communications, Eastbourne, England

First printing, 2005
Manufactured in China.
1 2 3 4 5 6 7 8 9 10 Printing/Year 08 07 06 05

ISBN 078144102-1

Editor: Heather Gemmen
Creative Director: Randy Maid
Design Manager: Nancy L. Haskins
Cover Designer: Helen Harrison/YaYe Design
Interior Designer: Patricia Keene

Dedication

**To the Body of Christ
at Cross Bend Christian Church—
For your *love*, your *joy*, your *peace*,
your *patience*, your *kindness*, your *goodness*,
your *faithfulness*, your *gentleness*, and your
self-control. I am nourished by your fruits.**

**"The Lord himself goes before you and will be
with you; he will never leave you nor forsake you.
Do not be afraid; do not be discouraged."
Deuteronomy 31:8**

God is there.

At the park the sky grows dark,
but we don't care — God is there.

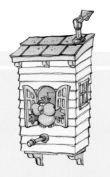

A breeze begins to bend the trees.

10

At the park the sky grows dark,
but we don't care – God is there.

Lightning streaks above the peaks.

A breeze begins to bend the trees.
At the park the sky grows dark,
but we don't care – God is there.

The rain comes down all over town.

Lightning streaks above the peaks.
A breeze begins to bend the trees.
At the park the sky grows dark,
    but we don't care – God is there.

The ride is like a slippery slide.

The rain comes down all over town.
Lightning streaks above the peaks.
A breeze begins to bend the trees.
At the park the sky grows dark,
    but we don't care – God is there.

A thunderous sound shakes the ground.

The ride is like a slippery slide.
The rain comes down all over town.
Lightning streaks above the peaks.
A breeze begins to bend the trees.
At the park the sky grows dark,
　　but we don't care – God is there.

We stand in awe and drop our jaw.

A thunderous sound shakes the ground.
The ride is like a slippery slide.
The rain comes down all over town.
Lightning streaks above the peaks.
A breeze begins to bend the trees.
At the park the sky grows dark.
We say a thank you prayer–
     God is everywhere.

God Is There

Life Issue: I want my children to know that God is always with them and can be trusted—in good times and bad.
Spiritual Building Block: Trust

Do the following activities to help your children understand that God is always by their side.

Sight:

Remind your children about a recent thunderstorm. Ask them if they were scared by anything they saw or heard. Then share with them about how God was with them, even during the scariest parts of the storm. Talk with your children about other scary things in life, and reinforce that God is always with them—even if things go bad.

Sound:

Talk with your children about how God is always as near as a prayer. Take time now to pray and talk to God together about any "storms" going on in their lives, and ask God for comfort when things get scary. Encourage each family member to take a turn to talk to God out loud and share their concerns with him.

Touch:

Ask your children to each find their favorite thing that they use for comfort when they are scared—a toy, a doll, or maybe a blanket. Let them share what makes this thing such a comfort during hard times. Open your Bible to a comforting and familiar story. Share with your children how the Bible is the best source of comfort when things get scary. Read to them a favorite verse that gives you comfort.